FOR MY SON, MICHAEL - R.P.E.

FOR MY MONKEYS,
BLESS THEIR TREE CLIMBING SOCKS - A.C.

my SON Lives

Ascendt Publishing is a registered trademark.
Visit us on the Web! MySonLivesInATree.com.
Library of Congress Cataloging-in-Publication Data: Pending
Names: Evans, Richard Paul, author | Catling, Andy illustrator
Title: My Son Lives in a Tree / by Richard Paul Evans; illustrated by Andy Catling
Description: Utah, Ascendt Publishing™ 2023 | Audience: Ages 3 – 7 | Audience: Grades K-1
Summary: When a father takes his family to the zoo, the zookeeper mistakes his son for an escaped monkey
and locks him up. The father tries to free his son but without success.
ISBN: 978-1-7376402-0-2 jacketed hardcover
ISBN: 978-1-7376402-0-1-9 eBook

(Library binding: hardcover jacketed)
Subjects: CYAC: Zoos–Fiction. | Sons–Fiction.

10 9 8 7 6 5 4 3 2 1
First Edition
To order bulk books go to: MySonLivesInATree.com

Published by Ascendt Publishing™
Printed in China

ASCENDT
PUBLISHING

IN A TREE

WRITTEN BY

RICHARD PAUL EVANS

ILLUSTRATED BY ANDY CATLING

A week ago, (Or maybe two),

I took my family to the zoo

The day was nice,

The sky was blue.

It seemed to me the thing to do.

No sooner there, I heard a shout,
"Someone's let a monkey out!"

I looked to see
Who caused this fuss.
The shouter pointed right at us!

And then the keeper of the zoo,
Did what it is, that keepers do.

He grabbed my son
(that rotten louse!)

And **locked** him in the monkey house

BANG!

And though I **stomped,**

And **yelled** with **rage**

They would not let him from the cage.

(go ahead and turn the page)

#free the boy,
I wrote online,
You cannot have
this son of mine

I fought for him, both tooth and nail,
To free him from that monkey jail,

FREEDOM

Free
the
Boy
or we
will go

FREE
The ~~monkey~~ normal Boy

But nothing I did seemed to help.

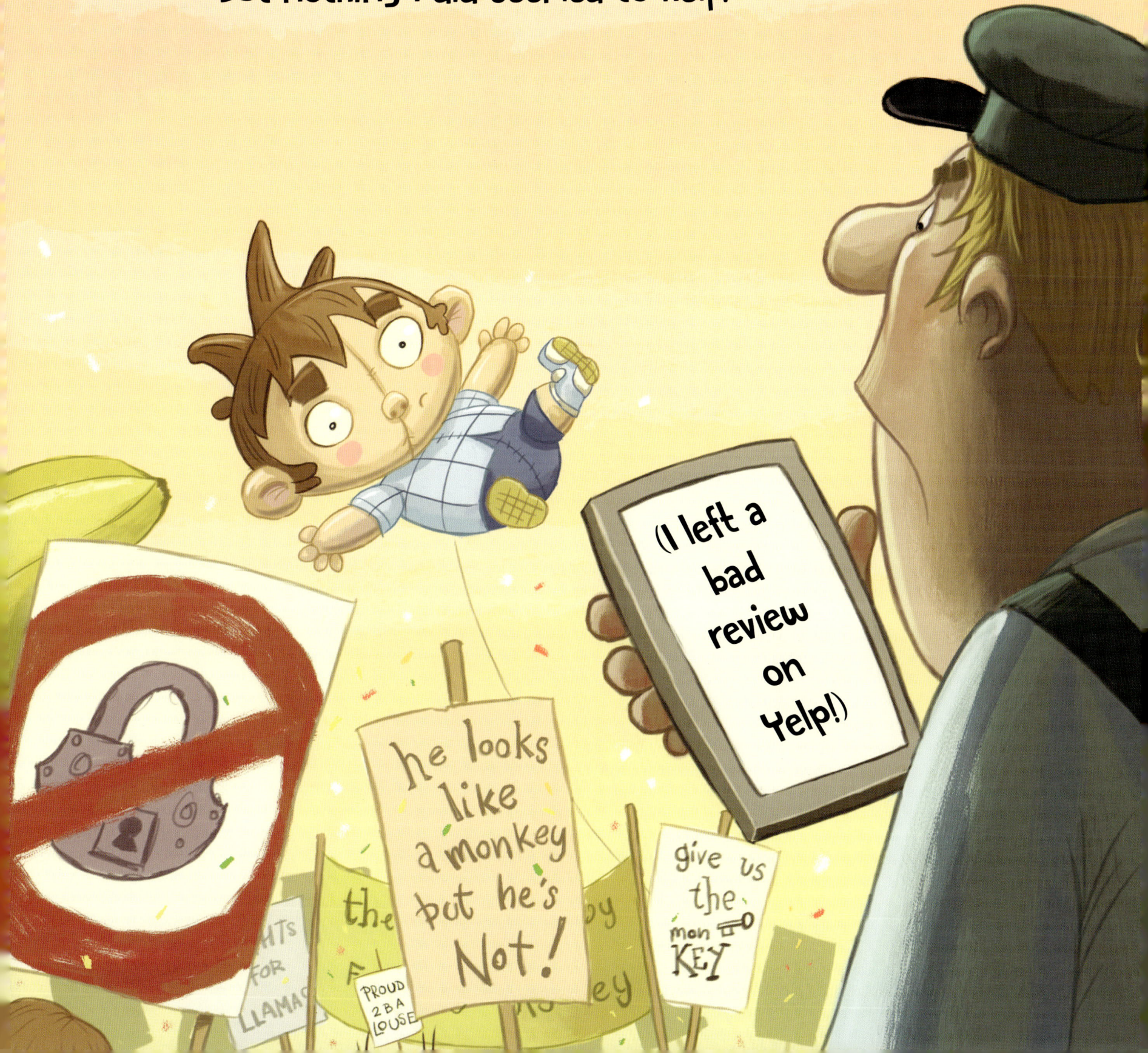

(I left a bad review on Yelp!)

he looks like a monkey but he's Not!

give us the mon KEY

PROUD 2 B A LOUSE

...HTS FOR LLAMA...

So, every day I went to see

My son up in that monkey tree.

Hoping that I'd get a glimpse,

Of my boy among those smelly chimps.

And then one day,

My son dropped by,

Swinging wildly from the sky.

To my surprise he looked just fine,

Clinging to a ropy vine.

Don't worry Dad, my son did say,
It's not so bad, I *want* to stay

"In here I do just as I please,
I spend my days up in the trees

and swinging with a hairy bunch
(we eat bananas for our lunch)

No mom or Dad (not anymore)
To tell me not to slam the door
Or wipe my feet or eat my peas

For snacks my friends
pick out my fleas.

hello cousin

No "where's your homework?"

"How's those grades?"

"No going out 'til beds are made!"

So, thank you Dad,

But I'm just fine,

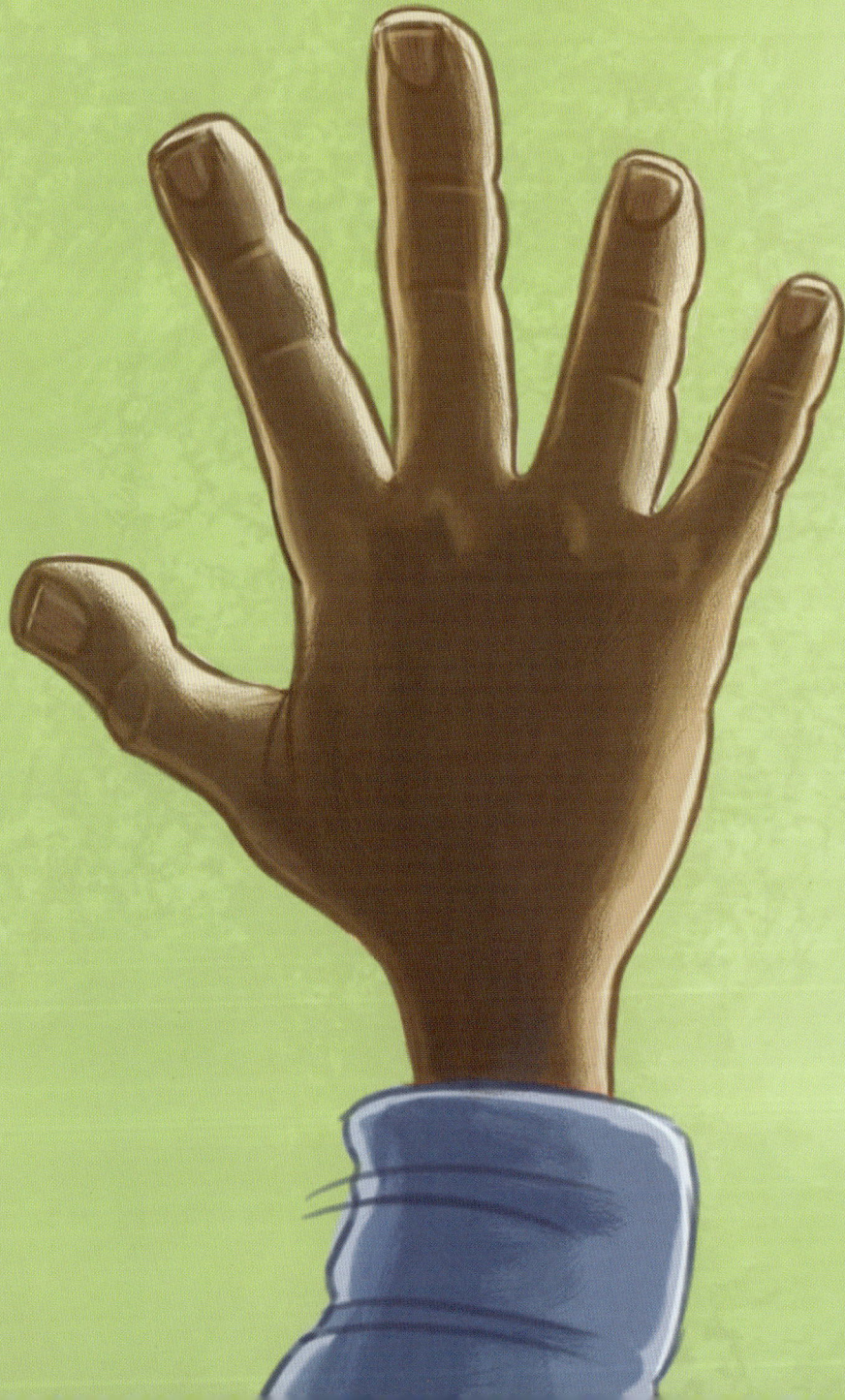

I gotta go, here comes the vine.

And that is how it came to be,

My son now living in a tree

I still don't know

When he'll come home

And that is why I wrote this poem

For though he says, 'It's lots of fun,'

It's not for me,

...I miss my son.

Do you see a monkey?